Dear Parent:
Your child's love of reading starts here!

Every child learns to read in a different way and at his or her own speed. Some go back and forth between reading levels and read favorite books again and again. Others read through each level in order. You can help your young reader improve and become more confident by encouraging his or her own interests and abilities. From books your child reads with you to the first books he or she reads alone, there are I Can Read Books for every stage of reading:

SHARED READING
Basic language, word repetition, and whimsical illustrations, ideal for sharing with your emergent reader

BEGINNING READING
Short sentences, familiar words, and simple concepts for children eager to read on their own

READING WITH HELP
Engaging stories, longer sentences, and language play for developing readers

READING ALONE
Complex plots, challenging vocabulary, and high-interest topics for the Independent reader

ADVANCED READING
Short paragraphs, chapters, and exciting themes for the perfect bridge to chapter books

I Can Read Books have introduced children to the joy of reading since 1957. Featuring award-winning authors and illustrators and a fabulous cast of beloved characters, I Can Read Books set the standard for beginning readers.

A lifetime of discovery begins with the magical words **"I Can Read!"**

Visit www.icanread.com for information
on enriching your child's reading experience.

For little sisters everywhere
and especially for mine, Jill Abramson
—J.O'C.

For Tamar:
Magical editor extraordinaire
—R.P.G.

I Can Read Book® is a trademark of HarperCollins Publishers.

Fancy Nancy: JoJo and the Magic Trick. Text copyright © 2017 by Jane O'Connor. Illustrations copyright © 2017 by Robin Preiss Glasser. All rights reserved. Manufactured in China. No part of this book may be used or reproduced in any manner whatsoever without written permission except in the case of brief quotations embodied in critical articles and reviews. For information address HarperCollins Children's Books, a division of HarperCollins Publishers, 195 Broadway, New York, NY 10007.
www.icanread.com

Library of Congress Control Number: 2015958384
ISBN 978-0-06-237796-8 (trade bdg.) —ISBN 978-0-06-237795-1 (pbk.)

Typography by Jeff Shake

16 17 18 19 20 SCP 10 9 8 7 6 5 4 3 2 1 ❖ First Edition

I Can Read!™

SHARED
My
First
READING

JoJo AND THE MAGIC TRICK

by Jane O'Connor
cover illustration by Robin Preiss Glasser

interior illustrations by Rick Whipple

HARPER
An Imprint of HarperCollinsPublishers

I am JoJo.

This is my magic cape.

This is my magic wand.

I can do magic now.

This is Nancy.

She is my big sister.

"You can't do magic,"
Nancy says.

"Your wand is a stick.
Your cape is a towel."

"Watch!" I say.

"I will do a magic trick now!

I will make flowers appear."

I wave my wand over a jar.
"Zippety zip!" I yell.

Oh no.

The magic does not work.

There are no flowers.

Maybe I need
better magic words.
I think up new ones.

"Watch!" I tell Nancy.

I wave my wand again.
"Bippity boo!" I yell.

Oh no.

There are still no flowers.

What is wrong with my magic?

Maybe I need
a bigger magic cape.

Maybe I need
a bigger cape
and a bigger wand.

Look!

Here is a magic hat.

Now I am all set.

"Watch me! Watch me!"
I say.

I wave my wand
one more time.
"Unga bunga!" I yell.

Oh no.

The jar breaks.

There is lots of glass.

Mommy runs over.

What a mess!

She cleans up the glass.

Mommy is not mad.

She says, "Don't cry."

"I wanted to do magic.
I wanted a flower
to appear," I say.

Mommy understands.
She gives me a cookie.
She gives me some milk.

"Look!" I tell Mommy.

"The milk and cookie are gone.

I made them disappear. . . .

"like magic!"